Picasso and Minou

P. I. Maltbie

Illustrated by Pau Estrada

ini Charlesbridge

To Janet and Brighton Gunter, for sharing
in my dream—P. I. M.

To Susan Sherman, for her wonderful friendship, inspiration,
and joie de vivre—P. E.

A full listing of the Pablo Picasso paintings that appear in this book, along with their locations and credits, can be found at the end of this book.

Published by Charlesbridge
85 Main Street
Watertown, MA 02472
(617) 926-0329
www.charlesbridge.com

Library of Congress Cataloging-in-Publication Data
Maltbie, P. I.
    Picasso and Minou / P. I. Maltbie ; illustrated by Pau Estrada.
        p. cm.
    Summary: The artist Pablo Picasso's cat Minou influences him to discontinue his
Blue Period style of painting to begin creating works that will sell more quickly.
Includes brief notes on Picasso's life and work.
    ISBN 978-1-57091-620-5 (reinforced for library use)
    ISBN 978-1-57091-648-9 (softcover)
1. Picasso, Pablo, 1881–1973—Juvenile fiction. [1. Picasso, Pablo, 1881–1973—Fiction.
2. Cats—Fiction. 3. Artists—Fiction.] I. Estrada, Pau, ill. II. Title.
PZ7.M29835Pi 2005
[E]—dc22   2004003302

Printed in China
(hc) 10 9 8 7 6 5 4 3 2 1
(sc) 10 9 8 7 6 5 4 3 2 1

Illustrations done in pencil, watercolor, and gouache on Canson paper
Display type and text type set in FiveOhOne and Truesdell
Color separations by Chroma Graphics, Singapore
Printed and bound by Regent Publishing Services
Production supervision by Brian G. Walker
Designed by Susan M. Sherman

Although Minou was a cat and not supposed
to know very much about art, he knew what he liked.
And he *didn't* like his friend's sad, blue paintings.

Night after night, Pablo Picasso gathered his brushes, paints, and canvases and painted the same thing over and over again—pictures of sad, blue people living in a cold, blue world.

"So, Minou, what do you think of my latest masterpiece?" Pablo asked.

Minou was too polite to let his friend know what he really thought, so he meowed. Pablo smiled and scratched Minou behind the ears. "The opinion of a true diplomat," he said.

Even though Pablo was poor, he shared whatever food he had with Minou. For Minou, living with Pablo was much better than being on the streets and looking for food in barrels of trash. That had been his life before Pablo had scooped him up and brought him home.

Sometimes, after breakfast, Minou and Pablo wandered through the streets of Paris. Pablo drew pictures of people he saw to put in his blue paintings while Minou looked for mice to chase. Once, on their way back home, they saw an old man begging. "Please, sir," the old man said to Pablo. "Could you give me a little money so I might get something to eat?"

Pablo pulled a coin out of his pocket and gave it to the old man. "I'm sorry, but this is all I have," he said.

When they returned home, Pablo went back to painting his latest blue picture while Minou watched. "See what a hard, cruel world it is, Minou?" he said. "Is it any wonder I paint sad, blue pictures?"

From listening to his friend, Minou learned that Pablo was also sad because a good friend of his had died. And Pablo just could not sell his blue paintings, so life seemed very sad indeed.

Even though he was sad sometimes, Pablo invited his friends over to look at his paintings. They were artists, too, and always had a lot to say about the blue pictures.

"You should paint something that sells, something happy," one said.

"People don't understand why your paintings are so sad," another friend said. "That's why you can't sell them. People are often afraid of what they can't understand."

Pablo got angry whenever anyone told him what he should paint. "I go where art takes me!" he shouted. "Everyone wants to understand my art. Why not try to understand the song of a bird?"

Many days and nights passed. Pablo kept painting his blue pictures and Minou sat by his side, watching.

Then, early one morning, Pablo picked up Minou and put him outside. "I am sorry, Minou," he said. "I can no longer feed us both. So you will have to find your own meals from now on."

Before Minou could run back inside the studio, Pablo shut the door. There was nothing for him to do but search the streets for something to eat.

Minou searched trash barrels and boxes piled up in the streets, but he could find only a few crusts of stale bread. It was a cold, cruel world, especially if one was hungry.

The smell of food led Minou to a restaurant. He slipped inside. But the minute Minou entered, chefs and waiters ran toward him from all sides. "Scat, cat! No cats allowed in here!" they shouted.

Outside once more, Minou kept walking. Soon, he found himself in a part of Montmartre that was new to him. People were dressed in brightly colored clothes. They didn't just walk or run. They jumped. They twirled. They spun in the air. One juggled several colorful balls and caught them all at once. These people were as nimble as cats, as graceful as butterflies. Minou was so amazed by them that he almost forgot how hungry he was.

"Oh, look—a cat!" one of the children cried out.

"Poor cat," a young girl said. "Look how hungry he is."

She gave him a plate of bread and stew. Minou gulped it down in an instant. "Maybe he would like something else to eat," the girl said.

She went into a caravan and came back with a sausage. "Here, cat," the girl said. "You need this more than we do."

Minou took the sausage in his mouth. He was ready to eat it, but then he remembered Pablo, who had taken such good care of him. Instead of eating the sausage, Minou held it in his mouth and ran toward Pablo's studio.

"Our little friend must be feeding a family," Minou's new friends said as they watched him disappear.

Soon Minou was at Pablo's studio. He scratched and scratched
at the door. He dropped the sausage and mewed. He meowed.
He yowled. At last the door opened. Pablo was amazed to see
Minou, and even more amazed when the cat rolled the big sausage
toward his feet.

A few minutes later, after the sausage had been washed and cooked, Minou and Pablo had meat for their supper.

"You are my one true friend," Pablo said as he scratched Minou behind his ears. "I won't forget this."

The next day, Minou returned to the place where he had been fed and made welcome. His new friends were happy to see him. Once again they fed him and made a fuss over him.

"Maybe he can join us," one boy said. "Imagine having a cat in our act!"

Once again, Minou was given a sausage. And once again, he took it back home. Pablo was always happy when Minou brought back their nightly dinner and wondered where his friend found such treats.

Then one day Pablo sold some of his drawings. "It isn't much, Minou," he said sadly. "But at least we can get something else to eat."

Pablo opened the door. "Come along, Minou," he said. "You must help me choose what we'll have for dinner tonight."

But once they were outside, Pablo changed his mind. "Let's go to the art store first," he said. "I'm running out of blue paint."

Blue paint? That meant Pablo was going to paint more blue pictures no one would ever buy. Minou had to stop his friend. He turned and ran in the opposite direction.

"Minou, wait! Where are you going?" Pablo called out.

Minou stopped and turned around. Pablo ran to catch up. "Where are you going?" he asked. "This is not the way to the art store."

Minou turned and continued to run down the street. He knew that he just had to bring the joy of his new friends to Pablo.

At last, they arrived where colorfully dressed people juggled balls and plates. Where they leaped and twirled in the air as graceful as butterflies, as nimble as cats.

"Look! Our cat has returned," the young girl cried out. "And he's brought someone with him."

Immediately, Minou and Pablo were surrounded by the performers. "Welcome," they told Pablo. "You're just in time for dinner," said the young girl as she winked at Minou.

Minou and Pablo shared a meal of bread and stew with their new
friends. A guitar was pulled out, and Pablo played it and sang songs. For a
time he seemed truly happy, for he smiled and even laughed.

"I'd like to paint a picture of you," Pablo said to his new friends,
"in return for sharing your supper with a poor artist."

The next day Pablo bought big tubes of red and white paint. "I need them to paint pictures of our new friends," he explained to Minou.

These new paintings were quite different from the blue paintings. They were gentle, peaceful paintings that made Minou feel calm and peaceful as well.

Over the next few weeks, Minou and Pablo visited their new friends many times and even watched them perform at the circus.

"The world is not as sad a place as you might think," they told Pablo. "You are a gifted artist. You can turn your world into whatever you want it to be."

A few days later, Pablo wrapped up a couple of the pink paintings in brown paper. "You must stay here for a while," he told Minou. "I want to show these to someone."

Minou curled up on the windowsill to nap. He awoke when he heard a key in the door and the sound of voices. Pablo had brought someone back with him, a much older man, well-dressed, well-fed, and not at all unhappy about life.

"So," the old man said. "Show me more of your new paintings."

Pablo pulled out pink paintings, one after another.

The old man seemed to like them. "Yes, yes," he said. "I'll buy these. I'll buy all of them. I'll even buy some of those blue paintings you keep trying to sell me. Who knows? If I hang them in my gallery next to your pink paintings, someone might buy them."

The old man had to make several trips to carry away all the paintings. And before he left, he gave Pablo several golden coins.

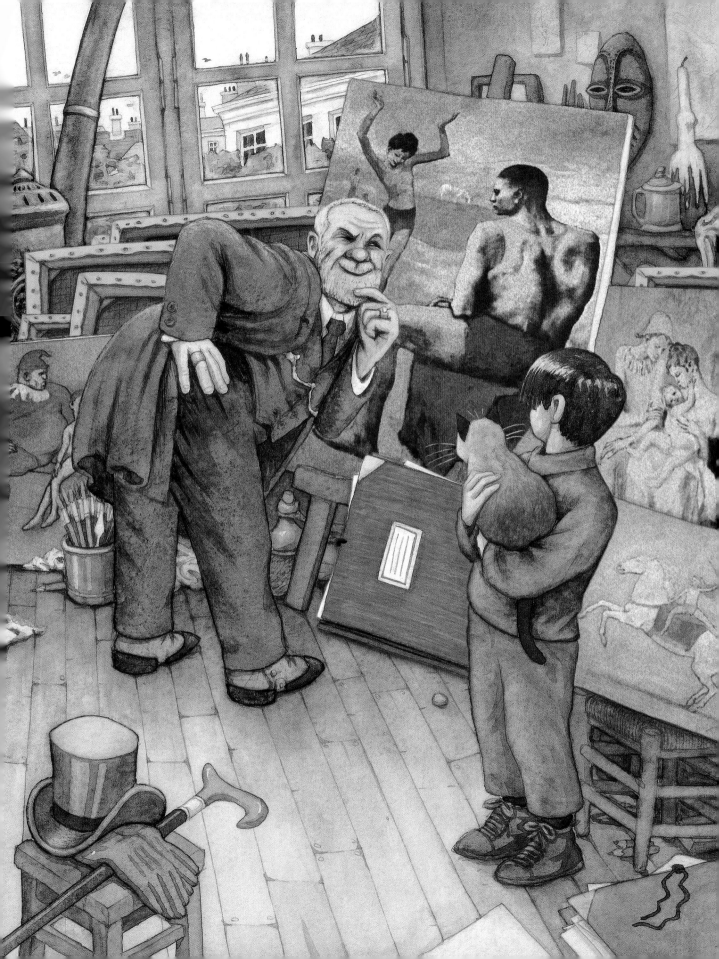

Like the return of the sun after a long, cold winter, the coins brought a big smile to Pablo's face. "Now we can eat like kings," he said to Minou. "And I will paint more pictures and sell them. Let's gather our friends for a celebratory feast!"

A few days later, Minou and Pablo moved out of their one room into a much larger and sunnier apartment. Minou felt the warmth and knew he was finally home. Now many people came to visit and even asked Pablo for his opinions about art.

Life seemed perfect. But after a while, Pablo stopped painting pictures of his kind friends. Instead, he started painting pictures unlike anything Minou, or anyone else, had ever seen before.

Minou was a cat and not supposed to know very much about art. But he knew what he liked. And whenever Pablo asked for his opinion of these paintings, Minou just meowed.

And Pablo smiled. "The opinion of a true diplomat," he said as he scratched Minou behind the ears.

Pablo Picasso, Spanish (1881–1973), © ARS, NY. *Self-portrait, in the studio on the Boulevard de Clichy*, December 1910, gelatin silver print, 14.7 x 11.6 cm. APPH2834; DP18. Musée Picasso, Paris, France. Photo credit: Réunion des Musées Nationaux / Art Resource, NY.

Pablo Picasso paintings and photograph: Copyright © Estate of Pablo Picasso / Artists Rights Society (ARS), New York.

Author's Note

In the spring of 1904, a young Spanish artist by the name of Pablo Picasso moved to the artist's section of Paris called Montmartre. Poor and unknown, Picasso could not sell any of his paintings because they were filled with sad, blue people living in a cold, blue world. This period of Picasso's life and work is called his Blue Period.

Living with Picasso at this time was a cat named Minou (the name used in France instead of Kitty), which Picasso had rescued off the streets. Minou watched as Picasso painted his sad, blue paintings. Then, when Picasso was no longer able to feed Minou, he had to put him back on the street. To his surprise, the cat brought home a sausage to share with his master. While the story of Minou bringing a sausage to Picasso is true, Minou did not introduce the circus performers to Picasso. That was borne of my imagination.

Picasso discovered the circus performers who would inspire his Rose Period during their performances in Paris. The colors of these paintings were mainly pink and rose, with some blue, and Picasso had no trouble selling them. With the money he made selling the Rose Period paintings, Picasso moved into a larger apartment. By then he was ready to begin his first experiments with a completely new style of painting—Cubism.

Friends and Influences from Picasso's Life

1. Max Jacob, Picasso's friend and a painter, poet, critic, and writer
2. Guillaume Apollinaire, Picasso's friend and a poet, critic, and writer
3. Chocolat, a cabaret dancer of the period
4. Henri Rousseau—nicknamed "le Douanier" (customs official)—Picasso's friend and a painter
5. Fernande Olivier, Picasso's sweetheart. In truth, she's the one who cooked the sausage.
6. Marie Laurencin, Picasso's friend, Apollinaire's sweetheart, and a painter
7. André Salmon, Picasso's friend and a poet, critic, and writer
8. María Picasso y López, Picasso's mother
9. Germaine Gargallo, sweetheart of Carlos Casagemas (Picasso's friend who died)
10. Jane Avril, subject of Toulouse-Lautrec's famous can-can dancer poster
11. Pablo Picasso as a boy
12. The Krogs, a Norwegian family of artists
13. Sebastià Junyer-Vidal, Picasso's friend and a Catalan artist
14. Wilhelm Uhl, a German art collector
15. Acrobats from Picasso's Rose Period

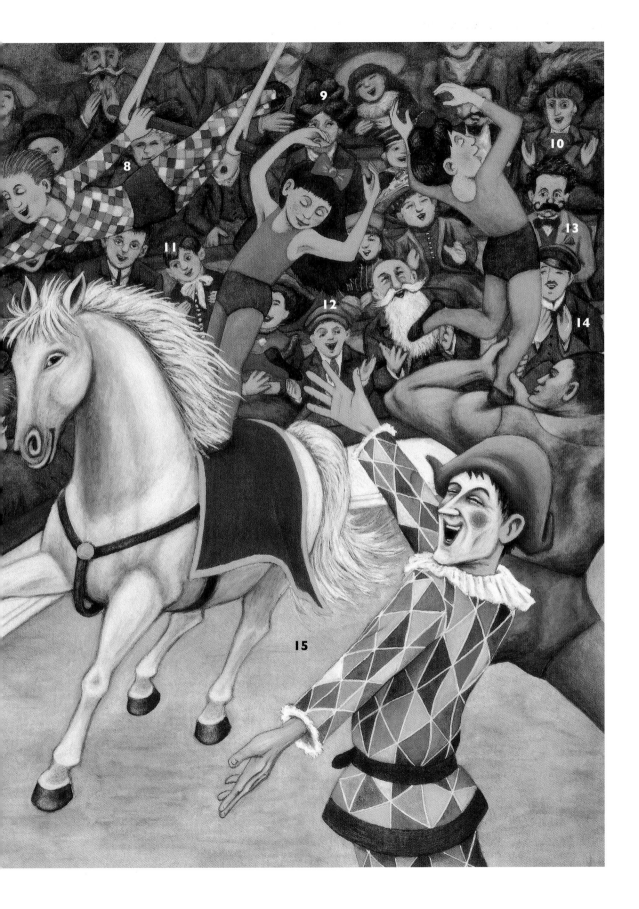

More Friends and Influences from Picasso's Life

1. Kees van Dongen, Picasso's friend and neighbor, and a Dutch painter
2. André Salmon
3. Max Jacob
4. Guillaume Apollinaire
5. Joaquim Sunyer i Miró, Picasso's friend and a Catalan painter
6. Sebastiá Junyer-Vidal
7. Ambroise Vollard, famous art dealer who sponsored Picasso's first one-man show

8. André Salmon
9. Gertrude Stein, Picasso's friend and an American writer and art collector
10. Alice B. Toklas, Gertrude's partner and a writer, critic, and editor
11. Fernande Olivier
12. Pablo Picasso
13. Leo Stein, Gertrude's brother and a critic and art collector
14. Max Jacob
15. Guillaume Apollinaire
16. Marie Laurencin

17. Minou, Picasso's cat (and an art critic)

The following pages show reproductions of Pablo Picasso's paintings as seen in the story. Picasso's artwork can be found in museums and galleries all over the world. To view more Picassos, visit your local art museum.

BLUE PERIOD PAINTINGS

Pablo Picasso, Spanish (1881–1973), *The Old Guitarist*, 1903/04, oil on panel, 122.9 x 82.6 cm. The Art Institute of Chicago: Helen Birch Bartlett Memorial Collection, 1926.253. Reproduction: The Art Institute of Chicago.

Pablo Picasso, Spanish (1881–1973), *Femme à la boucle*, 1903, watercolor on paper, 50 x 37 cm. Museu Picasso de Barcelona. © Museu Picasso de Barcelona. Photo credit: R. Muro.

Pablo Picasso, Spanish (1881–1973), *Self-Portrait*, 1901, oil on canvas, 81 x 60 cm. Musee Picasso, Paris, France. Photo: B. Hatala. Photo credit: Réunion des Musées Nationaux / Art Resource, NY.

Pablo Picasso, Spanish (1881–1973), *The Meeting*, 1902. Hermitage, St. Petersburg, Russia. Photo credit: Scala / Art Resource, NY.

Pablo Picasso, Spanish (1881–1973), *Old Jew (Blind Old Man and Young Boy)*, 1903, oil on canvas, 125 x 92 cm. Pushkin Museum of Fine Arts, Moscow, Russia. Photo credit: Scala / Art Resource, NY.

Pablo Picasso, Spanish (1881–1973), *Head of a Woman*, 1904, gouache on thin, textured wood pulp board, 427 x 313 mm (max). The Art Institute of Chicago: Bequest of Kate L. Brewster, 1950.128. Reproduction: The Art Institute of Chicago.

Pablo Picasso, Spanish (1881–1973), *Portrait of Sebastià Junyer-Vidal*, 1904, oil on paper, 56 x 46 cm. Museu Picasso de Barcelona. © Museu Picasso de Barcelona. Photo credit: R. Muro.

ROSE PERIOD PAINTINGS

Pablo Picasso, Spanish (1881–1973), *Seated Saltimbanque with Boy*, 1905, opaque watercolor and charcoal, sheet: 650.88 x 469.9 mm (25⅝ x 18½ in.). The Baltimore Museum of Art: The Cone Collection, formed by Dr. Claribel Cone and Miss Etta Cone of Baltimore, Maryland, BMA 1950.270. Reproduction: The Baltimore Museum of Art.

Pablo Picasso, Spanish (1881–1973), *Young Acrobat Balancing on a Ball*, 1905. Pushkin Museum of Fine Arts, Moscow, Russia. Photo credit: Scala / Art Resource, NY.

Pablo Picasso, Spanish (1881–1973), *Family of Acrobats*, 1905. Kuntsmuseum, Goeteborg, Sweden. Photo credit: Scala / Art Resource, NY.

Pablo Picasso, Spanish (1881–1973), *Young Horseback Rider (Jeune Ecuyere)*, 1905. Private Collection. Photo credit: Scala / Art Resource, NY.

CUBIST PAINTINGS

Pablo Picasso, Spanish (1881–1973), *The Dance of the Veils*, 1907. Hermitage, St. Petersburg, Russia. Photo credit: Scala / Art Resource, NY.

Pablo Picasso, Spanish (1881–1973), *Self-portrait*, 1907, oil on canvas, 56 x 45 cm. National Gallery, Prague, Czech Republic. Photo credit: Nimatallah / Art Resource, NY.

Pablo Picasso, Spanish (1881–1973), *Cruche, bol et citron*, 1907. Beyeler Collection, Basel. Reproduction: Beyeler Collection, Basel.